IRON OXIDE

SHOME DASGUPTA

ASSURE PRESS

Copyright © 2021 by Shome Dasgupta

All Rights Reserved. No part of this book may be performed, recorded, used or reproduced in any manner whatsoever without the written consent of the author and the permission of the publisher except in the case of brief quotations embodied in critical articles and review.

ASSURE PRESS

An imprint of Assure Press Publishing & Consulting, LLC

www.assurepress.org

Publisher's Note: Assure Press books may be purchased for educational, business, or sales promotional use. For information please visit the website.

Iron Oxide/Shome Dasgupta — 1st ed.

ISBN-13: 978-1-954573-24-6
eISBN-13: 978-1-954573-25-3

for Story F.

thank you, my friend

ACKNOWLEDGMENTS

"Weight Of Clouds" and "Flooded Sink" appeared in *Sí Señor*
"Seedless Oranges" appeared in *The Quiet Feather*
"Alongside" appeared in *The Fifth Di*
"If You" appeared in *Sylvan Echo*
"To Take Away" appeared in *Magma Poetry*
"The Pond Does Not Ripple" appeared in *Poetic Voices Without Borders 2 Anthology*
"The Rabbit's Entrance" and "Harnessed Above Earth" appeared in *Menacing Hedge*
"The Eroding Iron Of Memories Replenished" appeared in *The McNeese Review: Boudin Online*
"Path Of The Petals" appeared in *Atlas And Alice*
"Except For The Laughing Mouse" appeared in *Trouvaille Review*
"The Only Way We Know" appeared in *Cypress: A Poetry Journal*
"Bones" and "Know No Better" appeared in *Citron Review*
"Wander Throughout" appeared in *Parentheses Journal*
"We Walk Away Like Nothing" and "River Streams" appeared in *Emerge Literary Journal*

"Wild Wild Wild" appeared in *Clover & White*
"Maddened Skies" appeared in *Mineral*
"The Magnus Effect" appeared in *Stymie*

CONTENTS

The Only Way We Know	1
Wander Throughout	4
Sun Knowing	5
River Streams	7
Upon Arrival	9
The Way It Goes	10
A Layering Of Ghosts	11
A Reckoning	12
Know No Better	13
Distant Sounds	14
If You	15
Maddened Skies	16
The Eroding Iron Of Memories Replenished	17
I Know	19
Lime-Lit Orange Wonder	20
Speak	21
Musical Shadows	22
Path Of The Petals	23
A Welcoming	25
And I Wish The World	26
Farmer's Dilemma	27
Last Bloom	28
Carved Night	29
Unsung	30
So Said The Fallen Moss	31
Dance Of The Rabbits	32
A Million Years Ago	33
Smiled Like Rustic	34
Mouth Of The River	35
Speak Rain	36
Bones	37
Seconds	38

Threshold	39
Ocean Clouds	40
Regardless We Don't Care	41
Fossils And Shells	42
So Be It	43
Tap Tap Tap	45
Harnessed Above The Earth	46
Before Days	47
Soft Thuds Of Hope	48
Bellows Hunger	49
We Walk Away Like Nothing	50
Except For The Laughing Mouse	51
Wild Wild Wild	52
Seedless Oranges	53
The Rabbit's Entrance	55
Rippled Reflections	56
Alongside	57
Iron Oxide	58
Where Lightning Rests	60
The Pond Does Not Ripple	61
Flooded Sink	62
The Weight Of Clouds	63
Abegail Lee*	64
Saws Pipes Sparks	65
Swing Set	66
The Magnus Effect	68
To Take Away	69
Thank You	71
About the Author	73

IRON OXIDE

The Only Way We Know

Brittle the smile, gone went the grimace—
shallow heads sunk deep into a well
full of gone and gone, long done the thoughts:
past blocks—in shades and hues, imagined realities
once existed in distorted skies, fickle:
is the dance of the mind, and cloud cloud
clouds sang stretched lights—parallel to lines
connecting a tick tock world to haphazard
hazardous souls of belonged beings,
who once found meaning—of love and life and memories
in a stray mutt, tongue sagging, watery barks—
while searching for tasteless suds,
anything means everything when the forgotten
remember to remember: that they are the ones
meant to fade away into darkness, that is—
light we know but no longer want to exist,
and this, why geometric planes tilt this way and that,
plates welcoming maths of uncertainties.

Hoarse throats: lullaby of perception—
we are all so very gone, so very here—
time unaccounted for, but here here here:
just a moment, we reached out our hands
for skin for a leaf an orange a lime,
when sought a mud of ideas, that
once lit the universe, were no longer
purposeful—so we went our ways with a tongue
tasting of grit and smiles and a grimace gone full of dirt
and leaves of a fallen whatever truth—
so went and goes the matter of atoms, particles

of which we are all made but were never made to realize,
we're all so made to be confused: the end of it all
is just the beginning, and glitter sprinkles upon
our faces as if we know what really happened.

Shake shake shook.

All of our science: took the turtle's shell,
skull in meditation, chins are so up—
chins are so weary and worn:
worn was what we were meant to be—
glass, o' the glass and glass, glass glass sparked
the touch of ignition made to lead us
to a spiral of reflections and wooden ladders
beaten, eroded like rivers traveling
through crevices of our tongues
and taste buds and tacit towers,
soles of your standing: sound
and sound and sound, bells shout
like we haven't been heard for an infinity,
but no matter, no matter at all—we drift,
let ourselves unravel—it was all meant to be:
a silent understanding—it was never going to happen.

A blaze a fire a speck of ash:
swimming, stomach of ghost—
a specter spectacular,
we all should know—we are all that ghost,
the ghost that waves hi when we are looking down—
concrete cement coffins below, our souls
rusted—unwavering, fireflies once knew
what we were thinking—we never asked
for solace, we want but never seek—

a lake of glimmer settled upon our faces,
shimmer and shiver, it's all the same—
we've seen it all—heard, felt:
learned that the beginning is much like the end—
we're not surprised, not surprised at all—
in the end, we expected it to be that way,
and that is the only way we know

Wander Throughout

Gritted minds of holy spectacle jaws:
granted deep, in throats of wandering chests
breathe hard upon a ground like thuds of hooves
upon the body of earth, from a stray horse—
red eyes angry breath—stomped
fields of gleam, dew sing and sing
like a lost ghost in need of comfort.

We are all so together—we are all so alone,
green green green of all that exists:
in eyes of forgotten hope, when
we know the best is just a facade
of you and you and you and me and
we are of no good no good no good.

As brazen shoulders, heavy—pushed
down upon the tops of our heads,
yelps of pups in search of grocery markets
and yellow flowers: chewed mud, spat
out upon the open golden fields.

Of hay and metal—a tint of the sun
bent sideways: a beam a tunnel,
miscellany sorts of entrances going
deep through our eyes—in trance,
we hover until there is no ending, in
bits of sounds we wander throughout.

Sun Knowing

Cracked glass:
brown crunched leaves,

Sounds blend like one,
you step large steps,
shortened distance
between here and infinity,
where the horizon fades
into imagination, once
full of balloons, confetti, marigolds—

Sharp edges of each cloud
make sense: purple pink air,

You look up—closed eyes,
embraced sun, know
you will be cold soon, soon
your eyes will never open—

Inward you walk,
that one last chance, a search
to say:

what you really meant
when you said goodbye,

Aberrations, defined
by statues among the rest—

Rest easy the elbows:

slight tilt, the head, perched stance—

Closed eyes, a world well lit
with spices unfit for tongues
made for strayed minds,

angered maddened furious:
universe,

Shine, this aura sought
against lashed oceans,

A simple petal floats
against currents headstrong—
open your eyes,
see what meant not to be seen,

This—the beaten, the worn,
that, which was meant to be

River Streams

In which: the way we go,
we go until our eyes open
for the last time, until
we hold hands for the last time,
until the sun no longer exists,

The way the rain is slanted, angry,
sounds—rippled muds, eroded:

carved in a way,

Meaningless when meaning
no longer sought, wanted
meant to be trinkets, dashing,
flickered, a glow:
kept in splashed moments,
movements snapped: palms of memories,
when leaves—mystical castles,
fallen branches—wands of glory,

Remember the rust,
remember the grass,
remember the paved ways of the world
morphs into river streams, gleam,
under a moon-lit wild,

Cries of the night—
haven't the hollowed mouths,

When does it all end?

Half is only whole
when the whole:

half-met,

Where are eyes?

Dull dull dull,
a sky looks from below
where shallow ditches
yelp: to be deep,

Deeper, an entwining green
against brick-walled bodies—
long lost times when eyes
throw swirls, show:
withdrawn from all the rest,
we once played with clay,

We once felt to be worse

Upon Arrival

Wayward shift, so
the breeze ventures in:
an air of disparity,

Do you know?

This cut down oak stump:
We first held hands,
melodies of light heard,

Silver air so solid,
those dotted gleams of shine—

Marigolds upon marigolds
upon the crown of the lost,

There is the green, the yellow,
the pink purple, there is water—
there, blowing fields of nature,

Once found, now
only to float
with a wish, hovered
above, beyond the stars

The Way It Goes

Fire: solace—
pockets of fresh yarn,
an armoire packed, sorrow-filled:
sunken beams, particles
this way and that,
clavicles—heavy rocks,

Where's the moon?

Darkness grapples lackluster pebbles,
wandering, strayed—
strayed embers flicker—fly, dart:
stretched across sleepy waves—
bales of hay, land-ridden
clouds shift—acred minds, distorted
skies, a cardinal, a bluebird, a blackbird,

a flash of rain:

burnt ashed sugar cane fields,
this is the way it goes,
this is the way it goes
until the plates drift to find other lands

A Layering Of Ghosts

Golden streaks, striped
grand fields, endless green—
hay bales upon bales,
they look like life,

What do I know?
I don't ever want to know:

Wings in my head fly,
go, search,
a holding of hands,
sing to me—I'll listen,

Heavy is the cycle,
Broken:
the rest of the world
blends into horizons—in my mind,

A life without you or the wings in my skull

A Reckoning

Where there is no light—
an existence of looking,

Stretched out:

Drawn until trodden path
tilted blended bent,

Oh so lovely looks the ant,
this way and that—we
stare and stare and stare,
dirt separates, particle
per particle—personified
in palms of calloused past:

Wand of earth,
wields its way,
nothing understood
in between seconds,
in which we seem to exist

Know No Better

let beams be slant: let it be,
go forth boneless beams—
bent like bent like bent like twigs
so broken—core of world,
sun-locked shredded strays:
beams, bricks upon bricks
cemented in a mind lost by life—
what doesn't it all mean? when revealed,
slipped voices to recognize—
we know no better, between real and creviced
slits and slots meant for dew and sorrow:
so goes body of earth, world in itself—
let it be forgotten, for us—lost intangible skin

Distant Sounds

Cow's breath: spreads,
upon fields like fog—fresh manure,
fresh rusted yellow,
dinosaur long-neck—teethed, stretched:
a farm fleshed—full fresh bronze,
golden, dead risen—ghosts channeled,
fire-cracked sparks bellowed names—forgotten,
stray rabbits, mice survey future—
a deer: once a deer once wandered
like kingdoms, trumpets sounded,
loud horns of spirits—
split paths, together humbled blades
tilt, toward hoarse voices

If You

if you
neatly
cut on
the dotted
line around
my neck,
take my
head, and
place it
on the
kitchen
table,
and open
it up with
some pliers,
a wrench, and
a screwdriver,
you won't
see a brain.

there is nothing
there, except for
maybe a few
pictures, and
a lost memory

Maddened Skies

Mongrel beak: perched
atop a forked branch, drenched

Licked feathers:

Let all shine down
upon this world,
all of its shaken earth,

The catastrophe but to exist—
seek solace or peace or wonder,

I look up, maddened dark skies:
like scorned face, appeased tongue—
darkness brings light to trembled skin—

Perched mongrel beak:
if it exists after all,

And after all, the towers of leaves,
sparkle—leaves, a collage pressed
against rain, dark lit light upon
magnified gray yellow fields—

I look down, remember that one time
when nothing else was there

The Eroding Iron Of Memories Replenished

for Clementine

A sift through solemn eyes, the anger undoing,
A turn or twist of mosaic bark upon the banks of ridden rivers,

When twirling violet petals land, heavy and muddied,
When a pup becomes a striped stray kitten with ceaseless paws,

The mirage of sunsets over and over again flicker,
The puffed nostrils of a mad mad horse burning in twilight,

And the moon's shade, shallow and simmering,
And the moon's shade, inflamed in broken halos,

Surrounding sounds of distant thunder awakens, the clashing streams,
Surrounding the melodies of plate tectonics, the moving mass of dirt,

Where fiery harbors meet and explode,
Where the glittered beaks of the redbird's song protrudes,

For the splintered wooden souls entwined about like ice,
For the forked rivers sprinkling with steam,

And the ant pile growing and growing,
And the ant pile humming like bees, synapses forever tunneled.

Down goes the green green light,
Down goes the rotten blossoms of the shielded magnolia,

In which the branches find their way toward the mouths of stalagmite teeth,
In which the cackling bubbles search for searing homes,

Search search search for the flooding light, a thousand deluges in one,
Search search search the hovered skies full of softened lava,

Upon the jagged meandering of the canyon's edge,
Upon the sauntering of shadows, tinkering in a dance,

And find the rusted path to the past of swans and glass,
And find the calm calm waves, its tides washing the skulls,
And find the long un-grazed fields of bronzed weeds,
And the particles of colors combine to form the dome of splendid ashes

In between the cooling release of a palette of tongues,
In between the baby's heels, enwrapping air and pollen,

There the simple touch of tips and eyes, curling and wandering, and wondering,
There the eroding iron of memories replenished

I Know

where pennies drop down a wishing well:
i wish i was not there and you were alive—
the way the world looks now,

it looks sad and the sky is gone—
i was just remembering when you were laughing—

i am here now sitting at the bus stop alongside
a stray dog who knows so much more than me,
i whisper into its ear:

the world is such a scornful place in my eyes (because you are
no longer),
i'm just living like i care like i care like i care when there is
nothing to care—
i'm sorry, i'm sorry i don't know what to do,
you aren't here—just this sweet stray:
we'll sit forever here

Lime-Lit Orange Wonder

Stricken, weathered kind of day
makes for leaned sort,

Sides of earth, slide,
so wonderful into pores—skin
so taken, wanted feelings of words,
arms, eyes, so much means more—
speak ever flowing river winds

Upon the back, neck naked
amid lime-lit orange wonder
of dimmed stars, shining
lost tongues, teeth—

Folded leaves: best
for those who don't know

Speak

remember when you looked at me like i was supposed to speak and i didn't and the look on your face made me so sad if only i had the strength to say what you wanted to hear but all that you heard was nothing and nothing was never good enough when it came to us i'm sorry and you are the only person i know i'm sorry never more was there a time i would want to speak say something sometimes i feel like we are both ghosts this is when i feel most comfortable with you when we are drifting floating hovering in each other's presence trying to speak but only waving bye to each other in silence

Musical Shadows

Fickle—bent grass: toward sun-lit light,
shined shadows—across royal fields, so bold,
so arrogant, clouds shaped: mangoes—pears,
green-orange-yellow, back of earth: circles—
fire, halos swirl around and around, around
no voice: no wind, no spinning, a mailbox—
rusted, dented, bent—open mouth: tongue-less
seeker, seeking songs unheard before time:
why does rain stop? meaning: quiet love,
for space between drops, silence fills—exists

Path Of The Petals

Soft thuds against beaten mud,
horse's hooves, crashing red
breath, dying creek full of pebbles,
eroded banks, irrigated souls travel:

find paths—forgotten,
years from now, the way the petals
fall, sad and thinned, wiry
branches, embrace air, gleam,

Find nothing but nothing, nothing
works well when not seeking,

Circles, spirals—waves
bring the memory of us,

We were dirt clumped
together: all that we wanted,

The calmed horse sink its head,
The creek crept—sunken, wooden
arms like aged pastels, comes lit sun:

A sigh a neigh a beam of particles,

in clods, there was us,
Growing roots glowing:

heat and ash,

And nowhere else,
there is nothing,

Chlorophyll sprouts forth
from horse's eyes, outward
until there is no reach,

Traces of light
synthesize, twirl
within world's breath,

Engulfing us all
in an acorn of dew

A Welcoming

Years ago bark chipped:
like rust—frailed myrtles, tilt
toward earth, sink inward,
starved—thin, sad: fallen
heads, earth knew—welcomed
velocity, dirt roots lifted like
arched backs, up—tamed skies,
muted pasted spirits: foresaw
years ago, an ending so light
begins, between branched arms

And I Wish The World

i found a way to the core of the world it's in the space between you and i and i don't want to be here where are you and where are we the songs of sadness drift around in core hitting sides the boundaries unforgiving unrelenting lacking care for the melodies and notes written between each and every cloud cumulus cirrus stratus your face seems to real when i close my eyes and when i open my eyes you are not there and i wish the world its best standing at the wishing well with copper hands in between the sides of my skull a ghost i search for with my fingertips pressed against the air i wish you were here the core is unwelcomed not wanted but only the touch of your back and the voice of your ghost not lost but i stray away into the center of that which is not mine

Farmer's Dilemma

Mango tree: seasoned
ripened plucked—
string songs of fruit,
vary among fields,
a different tone—
A farmer's dilemma:
and so goes the wind
and so goes open palms
a whistle—a buried day,
shacks full of rust: unearthed
a million years, she trusts
her own hands, knots,
crevices—dug out paths, lead
to drops of juice, welcomed branches—
mangoes full of thought,
thoughtless: its surroundings,
they go into palms—known purpose

Last Bloom

Thus: the melted sky slanted over,
drooped upon our shoulders,
thickness weighs heavy, upon spheres:
there—a vibration, a slight shake
awakens enough: specter spectacular,
swaying waving floating,
thorns deepened into skin—the sun:
the sun looks upon its mathematics,
calm and pleased, there—the mule,
head down, hard breath,
blade by blade, step toward:
unknowing end, it knows better
not to know, A garden full of insects,
colors—final bloom: this, that lasted
forever, forever for all that was needed,
melted: beginnings—shadows undone

Carved Night

pale: night, darkness carved
around this bright clean plate,
there—nothing: splashed
stars blinked, laughed:

the sky was just a song
meant to be played mute,

sleeping limes,
so, the lemons,
not too far away:
a tractor entrenched,

a ditch, done and done

forever stayed, it bled—waterways,
the way of the sickle, retired,
hung on: wooden wall, swayed
when wind blew or door opened—
left alone—still sharp—forgotten,

the crops grew ten feet tall:
hugged night—a moon freshly bathed

Unsung

Violets look up:

strings of sky—
unstrung unsung—

We lie: between shades,
hands pressed—naked—relentless,

We whisper about violins,
how sad they sound
when alone, the same it goes:

moon, never ending—never ended,
Night: through channels, softened words
so quiet—maybe stems—maybe frogs,

We lie, there: skin against skin,
as if to say we're sorry—
sorry for everything, we mean

So Said The Fallen Moss

this the moss crept over—sodded
shoulders, a quiet place, closed eyes
equal infinity: nails, hammered tight
fitted, lost days the losing life, bodies
dead—still yearned for sunlit moons:

it's possible, so said fallen moss upon
graves of yonder folk, a bouquet here
a bouquet there gave meaning to ghosts
not dead, not living—not a choice:

a fight against fallen moss—
magnified by wayfared specters,
toiled ideas—gone let gone be gone:

floated lives, hovered like halos
over dead sought satisfaction,
searched open eyes: a beat
and a beat—thrived upon an ending—

once the flags of minds waved in slight
air, said hi or bye—and what else—
soothed and appeased: a lively thick of strings

Dance Of The Rabbits

fox—stretched under sky night—
silt thinned about, marble eyes mirrored
a moon full: river slept, quiet mumble—
dark red yellow eyes darted around
thoughts of rain and rabbits,
no wolves, this the day of reckoning:
church bells—distant, marked time,
fox paws, tail—lazily brushed grass:
a broom on cracked floor wood—church
covered vines, green purple leaves,
thief: waits waits waits—chimed bell,
then a slept town, door opened
—slick rabbits danced in darkness

A Million Years Ago

spilt dropped dew—
miles upon miles—
dirt prints puttered—

song of life, song:
a moon kept low, listened—
a rhythm, hum of stars:

breathed pale light, oxygen—

keys to dead souls, knocked
underneath, towered ahead:

palace for peasants dressed in straw,
born from greater beings, lesser
known—there the ant crawled
up walls in tune—spinning worlds,

a royal search, queen of piles—a maze,
irrigated paths—sought truth
under stolen ax, stemmed—a million
years ago: nothing to be conquered

Smiled Like Rustic

Shallowed minds guttered sparks:
speckled air, ghost drift float—
you once stood next to a hen
and I knew nothing else.

All I wanted to know:
pebbles of head rocked back forth,
made clinks clanks—sounds—
piece by piece I thought about.

Compass crazed flittered:
I couldn't shift my head but at you—
you smiled like rustic—
you smiled like metal tinged
against earth's horizon tears.

Years from now I will remember:
let it be known I was once tides of moon—
now nothing, now popped bubble
released into ghoulish realm.

Sighs regrets rusted acorns:
reminder: you and I were near—
you and I—you and I
separated, split bent crooked nails—

sorrowful hammer wooden moss.

Mouth Of The River

entrenched: dug deep—a core a chime a soft sway
in glowed blue tongues—mud reached, a beginning:
existence looped in darkness—shiny matrimony, nothing
the world's memory seemed: so weary the axis, tilted
toward sadness—graved cement, circuses entwined around
stems, vines curled—plates—crusts, spheres: crazed full stars:
river mouth, opened wide—awestruck wonder, a moon spark

Speak Rain

Across yawned lands: dim
lazy fields, bronze once bold—
there, a broken shovel aside grey clutter,
kitten—one paw up, shoveled sky: Once
was the kitten born upon its death, sits
now, unknown gaze—ear against iron-
oxide, head, a tongue in a tongue out,
in short bits sky covered anger, dark
haunted clouds—rain is to come—rain
is to speak, a dance upon beaks—once,
future queen yearns wooden handle
cracked like bone: heavy burdened stem,
drenched—a dew a butterfly, stung colorful
wings hover, like angel's halo over—
mongrel kitten broken shovel, that: once
a medium—to bury a dead forever

Bones

of what once was: clavicles
bonded by time, found
between red-yellow eyes, once
existed—howling heads of wolves, now
a mystery in teeth—over forgotten souls, so
goes the spin of the dirt, the twirl of chaos skies:
no yearn except for hungered skin, afloat—
gone and gone went you and i: we once were wolves,
our clavicles once touched, under
foolish beguiled rain, dropped
moon and like famished wolves we howled—
starved folk with pale pink tongues, furious
holy spectacles we were once

Seconds

lips like kiss we never spoke that was all we knew skin and skin stomachs in and out under a solace ocean full of dark dark dark i once told you about the time i loved you you were silent unspoken pensive is the mind of the loved you turned to me the moon was there like a guardian looking over us for once i didn't want a way out i wanted to be with you forever and forever it seems was just a figment of the world i once was lost but it was fine because all i knew was that there will be seconds when you would be gone i knew about that time and that time we were together knowing that you would be gone and that was all that i could ask for to be with for that time those seconds

Threshold

hollowed echoes
in pores, under
a sound so loud but to breathe in rain like life like wings like
bounced atoms:
let branches sway, let heaved lungs let lost the smiles of moved
clashed skies:
and to lightning, let lit the skin with fractured air and cracked
earth's skull:
quiet tongues
in songs, now gone

Ocean Clouds

somber mellow fields echo behind:
tall ghost green swayed grass—bellow
upon bellow—roofs, tin rust flaked,
away, years foregone: years away years
ago, fingertipped tongues: lost childhood
pasts—yellow shine: faded teeth, forth
twirled skies, dizzied lost, welcomed open
palms—faced up toward ocean clouds: once
was meant to be, meant to be all the soared
wings sang—under hanged branches, forlorn
sagged faced roots curled, in every which
way—away from us we lie: protruded earth, eyes
open—breathe breathe breathe: look, bare pins
stemmed, bark pricked air, for more more more

Regardless We Don't Care

heavy moss clumped clumping strands stray around soft looking soft feeling i kneel and hold your hand under the arched backs of acorns the milk lands bubble in sorrow the veins stretched upon each plain layers of fallen saddened leaves the moss sits stays gently as if there is nothing that matters matter fills our heads as we turn our arms into triangles pointing toward the direction we can't see amid black caved air seeping through our pores diffusion osmosis it can be regardless we don't care the saddened fallen leaves reminisce upon the onset of breaking day

Fossils And Shells

dented cans full of hay and dirt and torn photos denting inside ditches in between the scissor arms there used to be sunlit necklaces and bracelets shining sparkling like your eyes when the loud glitter bursts into mounds of colors spreading throughout the world's body like slow moving ghouls unburdened unchained unbeknownst the future hollowed and carved by slain remembrances of separated clasps of hands and mouths the cans indented into dirt like fossils and shells no longer meaning anything other than what was once just a figment of a cracked shard of a reality that found solace in a lonely embrace

So Be It

Your eyes
Your eyes
Your eyes:

Pollen from your pores—

my breath,
I breathe Spring
I breathe the poured rain, petals

honeysuckled from your glittered voice,
tongue of pale plated moons—

This shed of night:
you, calm and confident—

Do you know?
Will you know?
I don't know,

but just us,
under this mossy aged oak—

Will you turn this way?
Will you say my name?

So goes it:
a wooden boat full of holes—
ocean air of hushed tides,
frayed waves—

So be it,
I cherish
our unspoken words—

I cherish
dew drops
soaked in our souls

Tap Tap Tap

rain rain rain and rain lands soft, disappeared between bent blades half folded, folding toward whispered thoughts less than heard and starved strayed fields listen to gentle drops of sky, frayed lands pulsate beat echo boomed thuds and thunder, over heavy hooves and paws and claws, striped eyes see nothing but time in between seconds:

sun-tips and moon dance—a tap tap tap—licked mud gives in, soft until soared birds melt amid speckled horizon

Harnessed Above The Earth

stringed sounds come from the distance sky upon sky playing the world chopped down lemon trees iced and gleaming my eyes falter look away closed the twinkling clouds settle down upon the plains asking for rest hung low the stooped fields of glowing puffs ashed red the air around smelling the taste of yearning throat dry and swell the breath of the horse's hoof linger among the dry split leaves and go and go and go the day goes following the way the solo winged one ventures into deepened lines separating the world from its mirages solar ringing fastened tight around the clinging ropes the bells cracked and firm against the streaking wood harnessed above the earth

Before Days

Orange peels about dark green lands
sprinkled under dropped dew, winds blown
east against ends of world.

Mirrors shone over rock and stone: we walked,
we fell on our stomachs—breathed dirt
minerals like we were no longer human.

Pieces of earth here and there: magic
—wondered delighted touched.

Souls of magmatic cumulus clouded
mouths, coughed we sucked in—held
hands until our legs find better ways.

Soft Thuds Of Hope

down volcano swirling cauldron of soot and hay a frozen broth
seeks to fossilize the faces withdrawn looks and revealing teeth
time knows no bounds when it comes to tormented souls
dizzying around circular walls eroded and shook by the waning
layers of soil a lost mongrel with lowered head looks around
with watered eyes and sagged body brittle ribs and charcoal
gums nostrils to the earth in search of palms and sounds the
beating core weakens and lessens upon each soft thud a hope
nothing more than one more step amid the angry orange glow
of missing eyes

Bellows Hunger

Chickens strut

about nervous,

Broke clock—hands toward core dirt floors—
creaked wood, boards bend warped like
necks of solemn raccoons strewn in,
—barn door front, closed eyes—opened mouth,
paws tilted this way

and that

A call: from distance, distant
thunder bellows hunger: dismay,
wolves cows goats pigs—population,
one by one, decrease one way or another: all—
queens and kings and peasants

We Walk Away Like Nothing

how you slid your hair behind your ear:
a way the sun goes down below curved lines—
ahead, criss-cross patterns—dying grass,
a hopeless look under never-ending arches
of oaks and pecans: all its fission,
we walk away—silent calamity—heads full of sun's fire,
grounded balloons, deflated exhausted—yolk splashed,
yielded to day's fumes: yonder
mirages—ourselves, waver in mist
with flickered palms, facing us, as if,
a want to say hi, bye—fickle kittens
lean against broken glass rusted boards,
wait for diminished spectacles, into mouths—thinned field
pups with tails hidden in soaked dirt, we walk away like
nothing

Except For The Laughing Mouse

lazed daff-dils tilted drooped:
petals sagged yellows sad stems,
soaked fox tears—smoldered tongues
—smoke entwines teeth dripped with foliage,
peppered grey hum:

lost song the way the bales of hay sit
like they once conveyed meaning—turned
tractor, declawed—mosquito bit,
daff-dils rest like they're done, alone together
on stilts and twigs

—there is no bending—there is no standing
—there is nothing to be remembered—

except for the laughing mouse making its way
toward: speckled mud house full of ants,
spread about with no antennae

Wild Wild Wild

at heels of dawn stretched yarn straddles opaque skies unraveled universe it's during these times we question meanings of turtle shells and armadillos you and i we don't know if we're going to make it and do we care we wonder if the sunlight can shine the other way around as we tumble over ourselves over fresh raw egg yolk and ferns your wild wild wild hair tinges tips of the air around you and i can only look at cackling roots of frayed trees toiling over wooden chains surrounding us all lollipopped petals shield our thoughts from each other and we feel happy like nothing has or will happen a constant enthralling the world we amuse by our faults the plates shift this way and that tilting our point of views until we don't speak anymore approaching hopped frogs let their presence known by throats and wary melodies we play with thorns and let all else fail the only way to the bare road of twilight sprinkle

Seedless Oranges

If I could
dream, I
would be
standing
on the core
of the earth,
thinking
about how
I would like
to be in the
center of the moon:

in a castle,
surrounded
by dust and
the pitter patter
of gravity.
Here, I would
be laughing
with a girl
named Isosceles,
on the ocean
floor, while we
chew seedless
oranges.

These are
the reasons
why I would
close my

eyes, but
those are only
dreams of
dreaming,

for now,
until if ever
then, I will
have a brain
without
crevices.

The Rabbit's Entrance

broken scythes broken handles broken blades about the fields of what once was talking and laughing we gather reflections that come and go with the sun's shadow our blistered knuckles and palms our lathery necks never straight bowed heads the geese pierce the skies with their beaks the gathering of flapping wings and the sounds of horns vibrate the roofs of our mouths a lost meteorite planted in between the two trees where we first closed our eyes together mounds upon mounds of clouds stacked until our noses are vertical flexed crashing weeds litter and flow making fading puzzles out of the air a sad tale to be told we remain silent until the rabbit makes it way through the ditches of an unrelenting path towards clay and iron

Rippled Reflections

I understand gleam shine of sky,
streamed forth: vanished, a smile reflected
upon your face, there: a stream full of stars.

In creased pond—lily green,
I see your eyes—ahead: a fox stretched
across a thousand lands, a moon: a bowl
full of memories.

Remember?

We counted every raindrop,
every blinking rock of this universe:
we imagined with closed eyes—
spoken about with our hands clasped.

A rippled farewell: in washed
sounds—drowned in frog's tongue,
water swayed, this moment:
smooth hollow endless night.

Alongside

Into Saturn's stomach
we travel,

where organs and time
collide in bloody matrimony—

a collapse of reality,
in whirling motion
through the body.

The measurements are diluted
in the bile of a world,

where sound and vision
dissolve along with time.
Through the system of the internal,
the outside vanishes.

The dimensions have become a dream.
Together, we evaporate alongside
our reality.

Iron Oxide

My crest has fallen,
eclipsed and clipped.

This is the moon song:
waning with tides.

I breathe iron oxide
and wait for my body to chip away.

Evaporation is my life,
pore to pore, they disappear.
I look at my eyes
and wait for them to vanish.

No longer will I be—
no longer will I see myself among others.

This is not my belonging.
This, the existence of another.

Collapsing into air,
no more will I wonder about awakening or sleeping.

Gentle weeping will gently come to a halt.

Bit by bit,
thread undone—an unraveling of feeling stripped to purity of despair.

This, the last love song,
the moon song,
silently crooning with waves of gloom.

Where Lightning Rests

Sky: unforeseen,
enter—cloud's cave,
where bears hibernate
and stars try their best to glow.

Hollow bones—
where marrow dares to travel,
where lightning rests
until a clashing of air.

Follow the mountains—
they know the sky.
Be careful of darkness—
these waves know their own way,
but one incautious swivel:
captured in cloud's cave.

The Pond Does Not Ripple

Ophelia, are you mad,
sleeping in the water like that.

You can fall ill;
dry yourself, before fever arrives.

You look peaceful, relieved,
but please go back home
and have a warm bath.

Drink some hot tea
and stay under the covers.

What happens to beauty
when stricken with sickness
and turmoil?

Let us not find out.

Flooded Sink

You're a faucet that just drips away—into pipes, into tunnels, that lead to the eye sockets of the unknown, where concrete blends into dark mud.

You carry yourself on broken stilts, wanting to lean on the ground.

You're a ghost-town, full of drowning thoughts.
You drown in the rivers that lead to the edge of the world—a waterfall into space.

You can't float, you just drip away.

The Weight Of Clouds

Where shadows flow before my feet,
sparring with the clouds,
where above the skies, my thoughts fleet,
I breathe through shrouds—

made of dirt and grass,
the pebbles, conglomerate,
brings burdens of such great mass.
I stand still, and feel its weight.

With my arms rained in plea,
asking the green foams questions,
I bargain with the sea.
They have no answers.
I realize all is done,
the shadows are gone—

I am the lonely dancer,
dancing by the moon.
I waltz in craters and dunes,

where gravity is silent—
the moon light cry,
in the shadows' sighs,
I break and bend.

Abegail Lee[1]

Bright torn wind: feel never in wave-tomb my darling Abegail
Lee. Maybe open sea, a year ago dallow went I: tall sail sea—

throughout to see, sea
rise, by chilling moon—
where time beams for sounding love.

Loved her eyes—her: you wait in cloud dreams.
Her: six feet down, known kingdom apart,

I've water,
you'll then drift,

crash many stars moving you.

A spill: time sounding me never, end bringing tomb—
wait wait wait sepulchre bride,
wait for me by night-tide where I lie I lie I lie.

---

1. A cut-up of Jeremy Enigk's song, "Abegail Anne" (with permission) and Edgar Allen Poe's poem, "Annabel Lee."

Saws Pipes Sparks

wrenches and hammers   flamethrowers throwing sparks
welding metals steam rollers   moving like elephants
cows chew grass and banana peels   sounds of saws and pipes
echo   vibrate in our heads a machine of all sorts

Swing Set

The chains
broke; the
swing flew
from its set

and for
a few
seconds,
I flew
toward
the sun,

like a
rock
thrown
from an
angry man
who scorns
daylight.

Less than
a moment
later, my
head was
buried well
into an ant
pile. I did

not feel
their stings

though, for
my thoughts
continued to
soar toward
the balloon.

The Magnus Effect

And sound of wood cracked—split and splintered,
a hush and roar: how's that, they say.

And how this cricketer gone mad, shoved
his helmet and stripped bare—bat thrown six feet—
and when a blackbird flew over, as if to observe a spectacle
—how this crazed batter shouted one word
in echo and echo until reddened eyes gave way to lost tears.

As if there was no record he held
—as if he was no one to be known.

And in that one word, an existence
—her name her name her name.

A crowd and crowd, he knelt—put lips to pitch, naked
and dizzied and whispered her name one last time before tea
—one last time before it was all done, over and over.

To Take Away

I had a rock
in my shoe
but I didn't
take it out.

One day, when
I took my
shoes off, the
rock fell out.
I gently placed
in back into
my right shoe.
I liked the
way it felt —
the way the
limestone pressed
against my heel.

There is a
slight pain, but
I'm accustomed to

worse discomfort
than this. It

feels good — an
almost necessary
pleasure, almost
meant to be there

to take away
other silent aches.

THANK YOU

It has been quite a journey with this poetry collection, and it couldn't have been done without the following wonderful and magical beings:

Thank you, Mike Bourgeois and Andy LeGoullon—thank you so much, for everything. Thank you, Rien Fertel for being there, always. Thank you to my friends, who without hesitation, have always shown so much kindness and support—your friendship means so much, truly and sincerely. Thank you, Chad Cosby. Thank you, Karl Schott and Mandy Migues. Thank you, Luke Sonnier. Thank you, Paul Baker. Thank you, Jerome Moroux. Thank you, Sean Leon. Thank you, Clementine and Kitt. Thank you, Alina Ştefănescu. Thank you, Sneha Subramanian Kanta. Thank you, Lafayette Barnes & Noble. Thank you, Strangers.

Many thanks to the Literary Community who helped shape these poems and who provided so much encouragement. Thank you to the various journals and magazines who were so kind as to give a portion of these poems a chance.

Thank you, Assure Press—this is a dream come true.

And to my parents, Sarmistha and Subrata Dasgupta, my brother, Deep and my sister-in-law, Heidi—I love you all so much and thank you for traveling on this path with me—yes, it has been quite a journey. Love.

ABOUT THE AUTHOR

Shome Dasgupta is the author of *i am here And You Are Gone* (Winner Of The 2010 OW Press Contest), *The Seagull And The Urn* (HarperCollins India), *Anklet And Other Stories* (Golden Antelope Press), *Pretend I Am Someone You Like* (Livingston Press), *Mute* (Tolsun Books), *Iron Oxide* (Assure Press), and the forthcoming epistolary work of fiction, *Spectacles* (Word West). His fiction and poetry have been anthologized in *Best Small Fictions 2019*, and *Best Small Fictions 2021* (Sonder Press), *The &Now Awards 2: The Best Innovative Writing* (&Now Books), and *Poetic Voices Without Borders 2* (Gival Press). His work has been featured as a *storySouth* Million Writers Award Notable Story. His stories and poems have been nominated for the Pushcart Prize, Best Small Fictions, Best Of The Net, and the Orison Anthology. He is currently the series editor of the *Wigleaf* Top 50. He lives in Lafayette, LA, and can be found at www.shomedome.com.

 twitter.com/laughingyeti

www.ingramcontent.com/pod-product-compliance
Lightning Source LLC
Chambersburg PA
CBHW021450070526
44577CB00002B/347